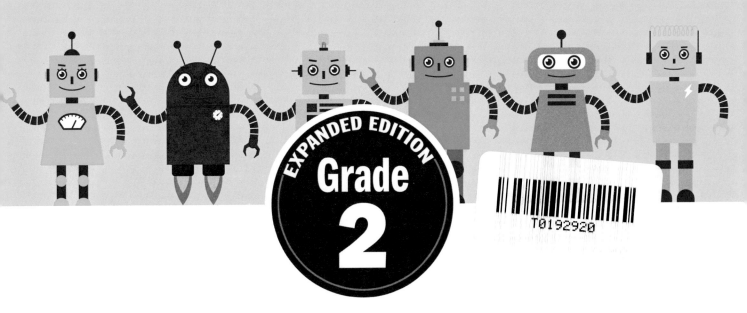

EXPANDED EDITION
Grade 2

T0192920

The *Melting and Freezing* lesson is part of the Picture-Perfect STEM program K–2 written by the program authors and includes lessons from their award-winning series.

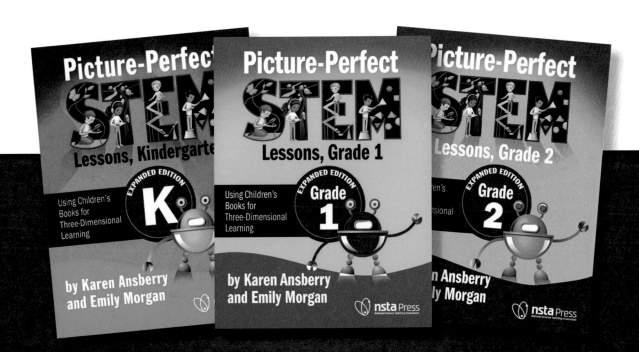

Picture-Perfect STEM Lessons, Kindergarten
Using Children's Books for Three-Dimensional Learning
EXPANDED EDITION K
by Karen Ansberry and Emily Morgan

Picture-Perfect STEM Lessons, Grade 1
Using Children's Books for Three-Dimensional Learning
EXPANDED EDITION Grade 1
by Karen Ansberry and Emily Morgan
nsta Press National Science Teaching Association

Picture-Perfect STEM Lessons, Grade 2
...ren's ...nsional
EXPANDED EDITION Grade 2
...n Ansberry ...ly Morgan
nsta Press National Science Teaching Association

Additional information about using the Picture Perfect Science series, including key reading strategies, NGSS connections, and the BSCS 5E instructional model can be downloaded for free at:

Melting and Freezing

Description

Frozen treats provide a fun, familiar phenomenon for learning about changes in matter. Through engaging read-alouds and some cool activities (pun intended) with Popsicles, students learn about liquids, solids, melting, and freezing.

Alignment with the *Next Generation Science Standards*

Performance Expectation
2-PS1-4: Construct an argument with evidence that some changes caused by heating or cooling can be reversed and some cannot.

Science and Engineering Practices	Disciplinary Core Ideas	Crosscutting Concepts
Obtaining, Evaluating, and Communicating Information Read grade-appropriate texts and/or use media to obtain scientific and/or technical information to determine patterns in and/or evidence about the natural and designed world(s). Communicate information or design ideas and/or solutions with others in oral and/or written forms using models, drawings, writing, or numbers that provide detail about scientific ideas, practices, and/or design ideas.	**PS1.A: Structure and Properties of Matter** Different kinds of matter exist and many of them can be either solid or liquid, depending on temperature. Matter can be described and classified by its observable properties. **PS1.B: Chemical Reactions** Heating or cooling a substance may cause changes that can be observed. Sometimes these changes are reversible, and sometimes they are not.	**Cause and Effect** Events have causes that generate observable patterns. **Scale, Proportion, and Quantity** Relative scales allow objects and events to be compared and described (e.g., bigger and smaller, hotter and colder, faster and slower).

Note: The activities in this lesson will help students move toward the performance expectations listed, which is the goal after multiple activities. However, the activities will not by themselves be sufficient to reach the performance expectations.

Featured Picture Books

TITLE: ***The Boy Who Invented the Popsicle: The Cool Science Behind Frank Epperson's Famous Frozen Treat***

AUTHOR: **Anne Renaud**

ILLUSTRATOR: **Milan Pavlovic**

PUBLISHER: **Kids Can Press**

YEAR: **2019**

GENRE: **Narrative Information**

SUMMARY: *A fun biography of the inventor of the Popsicle. This book highlights his scientific process, determination, and the help he received along the way.*

TITLE: ***Melting and Freezing***

AUTHOR: **Lisa Greathouse**

PUBLISHER: **Teacher Created Materials**

YEAR: **2010**

GENRE: **Non-Narrative Information**

SUMMARY: *Simple text and photographs introduce the states of matter and the processes of melting and freezing.*

Time Needed

This lesson will take several class periods and will need to be taught on sunny days during the warmer months of the school year. Suggested scheduling is as follows:

Session 1: Engage with *The Boy Who Invented the Popsicle* Read-Aloud, and **Explore** with Popsicle Soup, Part 1

Session 2: Explain with *Melting and Freezing* Read-Aloud and Popsicle Soup, Part 2

Session 3: Explain with Changes in Matter Article Read-Aloud or Pairs Read and Reversible Change Frayer Model

Session 4: Elaborate with Making Frozen Treats

Session 5: Evaluate with Make a Frozen Treat in a Flash Booklet

Materials

For The Boy Who Invented the Popsicle *Read-Aloud and* Popsicle Soup *(per student)*

- Store-bought or homemade ice pop on a stick
- Bowl
- Spoon

For Making Frozen Treats (per student)

- ½ cup (125 ml) fruit juice
- 10 large ice cubes
- 1 cup (250 ml) salt
- 1 cup (250 ml) water
- Small plastic resealable bag (heavy duty)
- Large plastic resealable bag (heavy duty)
- Spoons
- 1 pair of winter gloves or oven mitts (*Note:* If you ask students to bring these from home, be sure to have a few extras for anyone who forgets to bring them.)

Note: The supplies for making treats are from the book *The Boy Who Invented the Popsicle.* Feel free to adapt to fit your learning situation. To cut down on single-use plastics, you could have students bring in reusable water bottles to hold the ice, salt, and water, instead of using the gallon-size plastic bags. You can also cut down on the amount of salt needed by using rock salt (the kind used in ice-cream makers).

For STEM Everywhere (per student)

- 2 individual-size vanilla coffee creamers

SAFETY

- Check with the school nurse regarding allergies and how to deal with them.
- Have students wash their hands with soap and water upon completing the activity (before and after when consuming food).
- When making food to be eaten (e.g., frozen treats), make sure that all surfaces and equipment for making the food have been sanitized.
- When working with cool or cold liquids/solids, have students use appropriate personal protective equipment (PPE), including thermal gloves, eye protection, and aprons.

Student Pages

- Popsicle Soup
- Changes in Matter
- Reversible Change Frayer Model
- How to Make a Frozen Treat in a Flash
- STEM Everywhere

Background for Teachers

Matter is all around us. Matter is defined as anything that has mass and takes up space. All matter is made of tiny *atoms*. They are so small that you cannot see them with your eyes or even with a standard microscope. Atoms combine to form *molecules*, and these molecules make up a variety of substances. Most matter on Earth is found in one of three states: solid, liquid, or gas. Each state of matter can be identified by its distinctive properties of shape and volume. A *solid* has a definite shape and a definite volume. Its molecules are the most tightly bound together of the three main states of matter. A *liquid* has a definite volume, but its shape changes more readily because its molecules are more loosely bound

together than those of a solid. A liquid, whether it is thick or thin, is a wet substance that can be poured and always takes the shape of its container. A *gas* has no particular shape or volume. It will expand to fill the space it is in. It can also be compressed to fit a smaller container. Gas has this property because the distances between the molecules of a gas are much greater than the distances between the molecules of a solid or a liquid. Much of the universe is composed of a fourth state of matter known as *plasma*. Plasma has properties different from the other three fundamental states of matter. Scientists can generate plasma in a lab, and it naturally exists inside stars.

The *Framework* suggests that in grades K–2, students focus on matter's solid and liquid states and the transitions between these two states of matter—melting and freezing. *Melting* describes the change from solid to liquid and is caused by heating a solid. Solids have different temperatures at which they turn to liquid. For example, ice melts at 0°C (32°F) and chocolate melts at around 36°C (97°F). This is why ice melts at room temperature, but a chocolate bar stays solid. However, when you put a piece of chocolate in your mouth, which is about 37°C (98.6°F), it begins to melt. (Note: Chocolate is not a pure substance, so the temperature at which it melts can vary due to its recipe, but in most cases, it is solid at room temperature.) Likewise, different kinds of matter have different temperatures at which liquid turns to solid. For many substances, like water, the freezing point and melting point are the same temperature. However, for some mixtures and organic compounds, the freezing point can be lower than the melting point.

Making frozen treats with fruit juice in the classroom is a fun way to explore freezing and melting. The key is getting the juice cold enough to become solid. In the lesson, we suggest you place juice in a quart-size zippered bag and then place that bag into a gallon-size zippered bag containing ice salt. The salt lowers the freezing point of water from its usual freezing point of 0°C (32°F) to –2°C (28°F), making the ice-salt-water mixture in the outside bag much colder than ice alone. This very cold outer mixture causes the juice to freeze and become solid. Shaking the bag distributes the cold outer mixture so it makes better contact with the inner bag. The frozen treats will not come out completely solid in this process but will be more like a slushie.

The *Framework* suggests that K–2 students observe that some of the changes caused by heating and cooling are reversible (e.g., freezing and melting) and some are not (e.g., baking a cake, burning fuel). In this lesson, students read an article about reversible changes that presents examples and nonexamples. They use the vocabulary-building strategy of a Frayer model to make sense of the term *reversible change* and then apply it to the changes they observed in the classroom. During this activity, students are engaged in the science and engineering practice (SEP) of obtaining, evaluating, and communicating information as they read grade-appropriate texts to make sense of the concept of reversible changes. The crosscutting concept (CCC) of cause and effect is addressed as students realize that warming and cooling are the cause of the changes in matter they observe in this lesson.

Later, in grades 3–5, students learn about matter's *gas* state, as well as the core idea that all matter is made up of particles that are too small to see. The concept of reversible change in grades K–2 falls under the disciplinary core idea (DCI) of chemical reactions and sets a foundation for students to later learn about chemical reactions and the conservation of matter. Providing students with experiences with freezing and melting also lays the groundwork for what they will learn about the structure and changes in matter in the upper elementary grades.

Learning Progressions

Below are the DCI grade band endpoints for grades K–2 and 3–5. These are provided to show how student understanding of the DCIs in this lesson will progress in future grade levels.

DCIs	Grades K–2	Grades 3–5
PS1.A: Structure and Properties of Matter	• Different kinds of matter exist and many of them can be either solid or liquid, depending on temperature. Matter can be described and classified by its observable properties.	• Matter of any type can be subdivided into particles that are too small to see, but even then, the matter still exists and can be detected by other means. A model that shows that gases are made from matter particles that are too small to see and are moving freely around in space can explain many observations, including the inflation and shape of a balloon and the effects of air on larger particles or objects. • The amount of matter is conserved when it changes form, even in transitions in which it seems to vanish.
PS1.B: Chemical Reactions	• Heating or cooling a substance may cause changes that can be observed. Sometimes these changes are reversible, and sometimes they are not.	• When two or more different substances are mixed, a new substance with different properties may be formed. • No matter what reaction or change in properties occurs, the total weight of the substances does not change.

Source: Willard, T., ed. 2015. *The NSTA quick-reference guide to the* NGSS: *Elementary school.* Arlington, VA: NSTA Press.

engage

The Boy Who Invented the Popsicle Read-Aloud

 Making Connections

Show students the cover of *The Boy Who Invented the Popsicle* and share the title and subtitle. *Ask*

? What do you think this story is going to be about? (Answers will vary.)

? How many of you like Popsicles? (Answers will vary.)

? What are Popsicles made of? (Answers will vary.)

? How do you think Popsicles are made? (Answers will vary.)

? How do you think Popsicles got their name? (Answers will vary.)

Tell students that you are going to give each one of them a Popsicle. When they get it, you would like them to taste it (just one small bite) and then place it in a bowl while you read the book aloud. Call students away from their Popsicles (to the reading corner) and *ask*

? How did your Popsicle taste? (Answers will vary.)

? What flavor was it? (Answers will vary.)

? How did it feel on your tongue? (cold, hard)

? What do you think will happen to your Popsicle if we leave it in the bowl while we are reading this book? (Students may suggest that it will melt.)

CCC: Cause and Effect
Events have causes that generate observable patterns.

Connecting to the Common Core
Reading: Literature
KEY IDEAS AND DETAILS: 2.1

Read the book aloud, skipping the four experiment pages. After reading, *ask*

? What was the original name of the Popsicle? (*Ep-sicle*, because the inventor's last name was Epperson.)

? Why did the name change to Popsicle? (His children called him "Pop" and would say, "Pop, can we have a 'sicle?")

? What characteristics did Frank Epperson have that made him a good inventor? (He was curious, hard-working, creative, and didn't give up.)

explore

Popsicle Soup, Part 1

After reading, have students check on their Popsicles. *Ask*

? What does your Popsicle look like now? (It will likely be at least partly melted.)

Tell students that they have made Popsicle soup! Give each student a copy of the Popsicle Soup student page. Have them draw the Popsicle before and after it became Popsicle soup. Ask them to raise

MAKING POPSICLE SOUP

their hand when they finish their drawings, and you will bring them a spoon so they can eat their Popsicle soup. Tell them they will be doing part 2 of the student page later.

? Did the soup have the same flavor as the Popsicle? (yes)

? Did it feel the same in your mouth? (no)

? What was the difference? (It was liquid, it was runny, it was not as cold)

? Would it be possible to turn the Popsicle soup back into a Popsicle? (Answers will vary.)

? What would we have to do? (Answers will vary, but some students may suggest putting it in the freezer or making it cold again.)

> **CCC: Scale, Proportion, and Quantity**
> Relative scales allow objects to be compared and described (e.g., hotter and colder).

explain

Melting and Freezing Read-Aloud

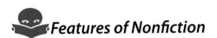**Features of Nonfiction**

> Connecting to the Common Core
> **Reading: Informational Text**
> CRAFT AND STRUCTURE: 2.5

> **SEP: Obtaining, Evaluating, and Communicating Information**
> Read grade-appropriate texts to obtain scientific information to determine patterns about the natural world.

Show students the cover of *Melting and Freezing. Ask*

? Do you think this book is fiction or nonfiction? Why? (Students might guess that that book is nonfiction because the illustration is a photograph and the title is about a science topic.)

Invite students to look for more clues that the book is nonfiction. Point out the table of contents, bold-print words, charts, diagrams, captions, insets, glossary, and index and explain that these are all features that indicate the book is nonfiction. Discuss the purpose of each of these features, such as:

Feature	Purpose
Table of Contents	A quick overview of what is inside, or an easy way to locate specific information
Bold-print word	Tells you that it is an important word (that usually appears in the glossary)
Chart	An organized way to share a lot of information
Diagram	Explains a concept through a picture
Caption	Tells you what is in the picture
Inset	Shares a fun fact or related piece of information
Glossary	Provides definitions of important words
Index	Shows the page number where you can find a word or topic

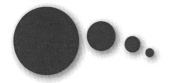

Making Connections: Text to World

Read the book aloud. Below are some questions and comments to help students make connections to the content being presented.

Page 4

Let students know that "ice pop" is the generic name for a Popsicle. (In fact, Popsicle is a registered trademark.)

Page 6

Remind students that their ice pop turned into a liquid just sitting the room. *Ask*

? Would a chocolate bar melt just sitting in the room? (No) Why not? (Answers will vary.)

Page 8

After reading this page about matter, *ask*

? What are some examples of solid matter in our classroom? (pencils, chairs, etc.)

? What are some examples of liquid matter in our classroom? (water, juice, etc.)

? What is an example of a gas in our classroom? (air)

Page 10

Ask

? What causes a puddle to turn from liquid to solid? (The water in the puddle gets very cold.)

? What is that process called? (freezing)

Page 16

Ask

? Most of our ice pop was made of ice (with some flavor and sugar). At what temperature does ice melt? (Find ice on the chart: 32°F.)

? What is the temperature of this room? (It will likely be around 70°F.)

? What do you think would happen if we took our ice pops outside in the summer when it

is 85°F? (Answers will vary, but students may figure out that the ice pop would melt faster.)

? Have you ever had an ice pop or ice cream cone melt all over your hand on a hot summer day? (Answers will vary. Explain that ice pops melt faster at higher temperatures.)

? At what temperature does chocolate melt? (Find chocolate on the chart: 97°F. Explain that different types of chocolate have different recipes, so this number might not be exact for all types of chocolate.)

? What happens when you put chocolate in your mouth? (It melts.)

? What is your body temperature? (Students may know that normal body temperature is 98.6°F.)

? Why does chocolate melt in your mouth? (Because chocolate turns to liquid at 97°F and the inside of our mouths is warmer than 97°F.)

Optional: Give each student a small chocolate such as a chocolate kiss. This is a good time to let students experience chocolate melting in their mouths.

Page 19

? What do ice pops and chocolate bunnies have in common? (Students may say that they are both delicious, but they are also made in the same way. They are melted into liquid, poured into molds, and cooled until they freeze in a solid shape.)

Page 27

? Have you ever made ice pops in your freezer at home? (Answers will vary.)

? What did you use to make them? (Answers will vary but may include juice, sports drinks, etc.)

? How and where do you think the ice pops we buy at the store are made? (Answers will vary.)

After reading, you may want to show students a video of ice pops being made in a factory (see "Websites"). Have students look for solids and liquids as the ice pops are being made and note the different technologies (robots, conveyor belts, molds, etc.) being used.

Popsicle Soup, Part 2

Next, have students complete part 2 of the Popsicle Soup student page by filling in the blanks with the vocabulary they learned from the book. The sentences read:

My Popsicle started out as a solid.

My Popsicle got warmer and turned into a liquid.

Changing from a solid to a liquid is called melting.

Encourage the students to take their papers home and explain to someone how they made Popsicle soup and read their completed sentences aloud to that person.

explain

Changes in Matter Article

*Pairs Read*

Pass out the Changes in Matter student page. Tell students this article will help them learn more about the changes they observed with their ice pops and other changes that matter can go through. You might choose to read the article aloud while students follow along, or have students do a pairs read. In a pairs read, students take turns reading aloud to each other. While one person reads a paragraph, the other listens and makes comments ("I think …"), asks questions ("I wonder …"), or shares new learnings ("I didn't know …").

Revisit *Melting and Freezing* to look for examples of reversible changes in the photos, such as:

- An ice pop melting (can be frozen into an ice pop again)
- Chocolate melting (can be cooled into solid chocolate again)
- A pond freezing (will melt into a liquid pond when the temperature rises)
- Chocolate cooling into a bunny shape (can be melted into liquid chocolate and made into a different shape)
- Icicles freezing on a fountain (will melt when the temperature rises)

Ask

? What are some examples of changes that are not reversible? (Frying an egg, because it can't be turned back into a liquid egg. Burning paper, because it turns into something else—ash and smoke. It can't be turned back into paper.)

Reversible Change Frayer Model

*Frayer Model*

Next, give each student a copy of the Reversible Change Frayer Model student page. Students can use the information they learn from the article to complete the Frayer Model. The Frayer Model is a tool to help students develop their vocabularies by studying concepts in a relational manner. Students write a particular word in the middle of a box and proceed to include drawings, examples, nonexamples, and a definition in other quadrants of the box. They can proceed by using the examples and characteristics to help them formulate a definition or, conversely, by using the definition to

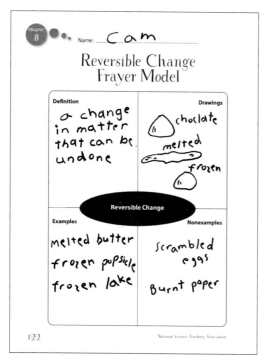

Chapter 8   Name: _Cam_

Reversible Change Frayer Model

Definition	Drawings
a change in matter that can be undone	choclate melted frozen

Reversible Change

Examples	Nonexamples
melted butter frozen popsicle frozen lake	scrambled eggs Burnt paper

122   National Science Teaching Association

FRAYER MODEL

determine examples and nonexamples. In this case, have students use the preceding article to formulate a definition for *reversible change* in their own words in the top left box of the Reversible Change Frayer Model student page. Then have students write some characteristics of reversible changes in the top right box. Have students work in pairs to come up with examples and nonexamples from their own lives. As you observe students working, encourage them to use their previous experiences as a basis for their reversible change examples. Students can then present and explain their Frayer Models to other groups. As they present to one another, informally assess their understanding of the concept and clarify as necessary.

*e*laborate

Making Frozen Treats

In advance of this activity, ask each student to bring in a pair of winter gloves or oven mitts.

Ask

? How did Frank Epperson get his Popsicles to freeze quickly? (He added salt to lower the freezing point of the water so the Popsicles would get colder faster.)

? Do you think we could use that process to make a frozen treat right here in our classroom? (Answers will vary depending on if you have a freezer.)

? What materials do you think we would need? (Answers will vary.)

Have students explain their reasoning for each material or ingredient they suggest. Then show students page 21 of *The Boy Who Invented the Popsicle*, titled "A Frozen Treat in a Flash." Tell them that they can follow these instructions to make a frozen treat in only five minutes!

Note: You may want to have parent volunteers help out, or invite some older student "buddies" to help. If you are not able to get assistance, you can adapt this activity to be a demonstration.

MAKING A FROZEN TREAT IN A FLASH

Gather the materials listed on page 31 (also in the materials section of this lesson) and instruct students to follow these instructions (modified from page 31):

1. Pour ½ cup (125 ml) of juice into the small plastic bag. Seal the bag, trying to remove as much air as possible.

2. Pour the ice cubes, water, and salt into the large plastic bag.

3. Put the small bag into the large bag. Seal the large bag, and make sure it is tightly sealed.

4. Put on gloves and shake the bag back and forth for about five minutes to mix the ice, water, and salt around the small bag. (You may want play a song during this time.)

5. After five minutes, open the large bag and take out the small bag. Wipe off the salt water from the small bag and dispose of the large bag. (Students may need assistance.)

Give each student a spoon and allow them to eat their frozen treat!

Read the explanation titled "What happened?" on page 31 of *The Boy Who Invented the Popsicle* and *ask*

? Why did we add salt to the ice and water mixture? (The salt lowers the freezing point of water, making the water much colder than 32°F. This made the treat freeze faster.)

If you have access to a freezer, you could place ½ cup of juice in a plastic bag for five minutes to show how it does not freeze as fast as when the salt was added to the mixture of ice and water. *Ask*

? Was this a reversible change? (yes)

? Why? (Because you can turn it back into liquid juice by letting it warm up.)

While students enjoy their frozen treats, show some videos of Popsicles being made in factories (see "Websites"). They can compare the processes in the videos to the process they used to make their frozen treats.

evaluate

Make a Frozen Treat in a Flash Booklet

 *Writing*

Connecting to the Common Core
Writing
RESEARCH TO BUILD AND PRESENT KNOWLEDGE: 2.7
Language
VOCABULARY ACQUISITION AND USE: 2.6

SEP: Obtaining, Evaluating, and Communicating Information
Communicate information with others in written forms using drawings and writing that provide detail about scientific ideas.

Give each student a copy of the How to Make a Frozen Treat in a Flash student pages. Have each student write the correct word to complete each sentence and then illustrate each sentence in the box. Encourage students to go back to each page and add more details. For example, the sentences should read:

First, place liquid juice in the small plastic bag.

Next, add solid ice and salt to the large plastic bag.

The salt lowers the temperature of the ice so the treat can freeze faster.

Then place the small bag into the large bag. Shake the large bag to turn the liquid in the small bag into a solid.

Last, take the solid treat out of the bag and eat it before it melts. Remember, this is a reversible change. If it melts, you can freeze it again!

STEM Everywhere

Give students the STEM Everywhere student page as a way to involve their families and extend their learning. They can do the activity with an adult helper and share their results with the class. You will need to send home two individual coffee creamers with each student for this activity.

Opportunities for Differentiated Instruction

This box lists questions and challenges related to the lesson that students may select to research, investigate, or innovate. Students may also use the questions as examples to help them generate their own questions. These questions can help you move your students from the teacher-directed investigation to engaging in the science and engineering practices in a more student-directed format.

Extra Support

For students who are struggling to meet the lesson objectives, provide a question and guide them in the process of collecting research or help them design procedures or solutions.

Extensions

For students with high interest or who have already met the lesson objectives, have them choose a question (or pose their own question), conduct their own research, and design their own procedures or solutions.

After selecting one of the questions in the box or formulating their own question, students can individually or collaboratively make predictions, design investigations or surveys to test their predictions, collect evidence, devise explanations, design solutions, or examine related resources. They can communicate their findings through a science notebook, at a poster session or gallery walk, or by producing a media project.

Research

Have students brainstorm researchable questions:

? How do the melting points of various substances compare? Make a chart!

? How is ice cream made?

? How do companies keep ice pops and ice-cream bars from melting when they ship them to stores?

Continued

Opportunities for Differentiated Instruction (*continued*)

Investigate

Have students brainstorm testable questions to be solved through science or math:

? How does the volume of liquid water change when you freeze it?

? What is your class's favorite flavor of ice pop? Take a survey!

? Does the amount of a liquid affect how fast it freezes?

Innovate

Have students brainstorm problems to be solved through engineering:

? Can you design something to keep an ice cube from melting?

? Can you design something to make an ice cube melt quickly?

? Can you come up with a recipe for a new frozen treat?

Websites

 How Twin Pops are Made: The Ziegenfelder Company
www.youtube.com/ watch?v=y02TBgkBUhg

 How Red White and Blue Pops are Made
www.youtube.com/ watch?v=P2hCDq2qUrk

 Ice Pop Manufacturing at the Ice Pop Factory
www.youtube.com/ watch?v=GLFQRmWJadY

More Books to Read

Boothroyd, J. 2011. *Many kinds of matter: A look at solids, liquids, and gases.* New York: Lerner
Summary: Full-color photographs and simple text provide everyday examples of solids, liquids, and gases.

Diehn, A. 2018. *Matter: Physical science for kids.* White River Junction, VT: Nomad Press.
Summary: From the Picture Book Science series, this book provides a simple definition of *matter*, information on the states of matter, and examples of things that are not matter.

Hansen, A. 2011. *Matter comes in all shapes.* Vero Beach, FL: Rourke Educational Media.
Summary: Simple text and photographs explain the differences between solids, liquids, and gases.

Hansen, A. 2011. *Solid or liquid?* Vero Beach, FL: Rourke Educational Media.
Summary: Simple text and photographs explain the differences between solids and liquids.

Mason, A. 2006. *Change it!: Solids, liquids, gases and you.* Toronto: Kids Can Press.
Summary: Filled with information and activities, this book provides a simple introduction to the states of matter.

Willems, M. 2011. *Should I share my ice cream?* New York: Hyperion Books for Children.
Summary: From the Elephant and Piggie series, this book follows Gerald the elephant as he makes a big decision: Should he share his ice cream? He waits too long and it melts, but Piggie brings more and saves the day.

Zoehfeld, K. W. 2015. *What is the world made of?: All about solids, liquids, and gases.* New York: Harper-Collins.
Summary: From the Let's-Read-and-Find-Out Science series, this book gives examples of each state of matter and some simple activities that demonstrate the attributes of each.

Popsicle Soup

Part 1

Draw a picture of your Popsicle before and after it became Popsicle soup in the boxes below:

Before   **After**

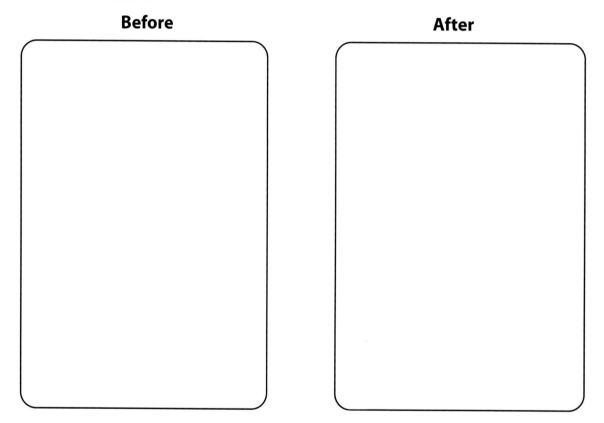

Part 2

My Popsicle started out as a _____.
(solid or liquid)

My Popsicle got warmer and turned into a _____.
(solid or liquid)

Changing from a solid to a liquid is called _____.
(freezing or melting)

Changes in Matter

Reversible Changes

Heating or cooling matter can cause it to change. A reversible change is a change in matter that can be reversed, or undone. Melting and freezing are usually reversible changes. For example, if you add heat to solid butter, it can melt and change into a liquid. Once the butter is liquid, the change can be reversed. You can change it back into solid butter by cooling it.

Freezing and Melting

Different kinds of matter freeze and melt at different temperatures. For example, a piece of chocolate will begin to melt into a liquid at around 97°F. If it cools to below 97°F, it will begin to form a solid again. You can melt and freeze a piece of chocolate over and over again because it is a reversible change.

Liquid water freezes at 32°F and becomes ice. When the temperature of ice rises above 32°F, it begins to melt and become liquid water again. You can freeze and melt water over and over because it is a reversible change.

Are All Changes Reversible?

If you crack a raw egg, you will find that it is mostly liquid inside. When you add enough heat to cook the egg, it becomes a solid. But cooking an egg is NOT a reversible change. You can't make the egg liquid again!

If you burn a piece of paper, it changes. It turns into ashes and smoke. It is not paper anymore. It cannot go back to what it was before. So not all changes are reversible!

When the leaf of a plant gets too cold, it can freeze. It can become hard and stiff. When the leaf warms up, it cannot go back to what it was before. So this is NOT a reversible change.

You can cause changes in matter by heating or cooling it. Some of these changes can be reversed and some cannot. Can you think of more examples of reversible changes?

Reversible Change
Frayer Model

Definition	Drawings

Reversible Change

Examples	Nonexamples

National Science Teaching Association

How to Make
a Frozen Treat
in a Flash

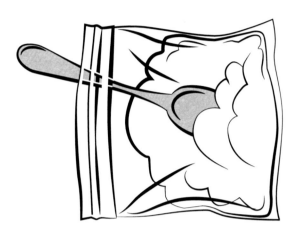

Name: _____

Last, take the treat out of the bag and eat it before
it _____ .
   (melts or freezes)

[large blank box]

Remember, this is _____ change.
   (a reversible or not a reversible)

If it melts, you can freeze it again!

First, place the _____ juice in
(solid or liquid)
a small plastic bag.

Next, add _____ ice and salt to
(solid or liquid)
the large plastic bag.

The salt lowers the temperature of the ice so the
treat can _____ faster.
(melt or freeze)

Then place the small bag into the large bag.
Shake to turn the liquid in the small bag into a
_____.
(solid or liquid)

National Science Teaching Association

Name: _____

STEM Everywhere

Dear Families,

At school, we have been learning about **melting and freezing**. We made Popsicle soup and a frozen treat. We learned that melting and freezing are reversible changes. We also learned that salt can be used to make things freeze faster. Why do we salt sidewalks? To find out more, ask your learner questions such as:

- What did you learn?
- What was your favorite part of the lesson?
- What are you still wondering?

At home, you can turn liquid coffee creamer into solid ice cream with the help of some ice and salt. Follow the instructions below.

Materials
2 vanilla coffee creamers (individual size)
Reusable water bottle or container with tight lid
Ice to fill container
¼ cup of salt
Water

Instructions
1. Place your creamer cups in the bottle.
2. Fill your bottle ½ full with ice.
3. Add ¼ cup salt.
4. Fill the rest of the bottle with ice.
5. Add water until about ½ full.
6. Place the lid tightly on your container.
7. Shake the bottle for five minutes. (You may want to wear gloves or oven mitts as the bottle will get very cold.)
8. Remove the creamer and, without opening it, check to see if it is solid by either squeezing the sides or shaking the cup near your ear. If you feel or hear liquid, place the creamer cups back in the bottle and shake for two more minutes.
9. Open and enjoy!